These are Good Poems!

These are Good Poems!
Copyright © Eugene S. Cuny 2021
All Rights Reserved
Published by Kallisto Gaia Press Inc.
First Edition

No part of this book may be used or reproduced in any manner without written permision except in the case of brief quotations embodied in critical articles or reviews.

Kallisto Gaia Press Inc.
801 E. 51st Street
Suite 365-246
Austin TX 78723
Phone (254) 654-7205
www.Kallistogaiapress.org

ISBN: 978-1-952224-10-2

These are Good Poems!

E.S. Cuny

for

Patricia

Table of Contents

These Are Good Poems!	1
How It Goes	3
Ode to Daily Routine	4
Jigsaws	5
Ode to Cernan	6
Black Holes I Have Known	7
Of Mystery and Substance	8
Some Mornings!	10
The Church of the Flying Tube	11
The Blackened Heart of Hypocrisy	13
How a Ghost Sees Things	16
Parisian Orpheunium	17
Poetry Webinair	18
When It's Gettin' Hot In Texas	20
With a Wink	22
Cornucopias I Have Known	24
Things Return To Place	25

These Are Good Poems!

You can tell because they have rhymes
      and even rhythm –
(at least sometimes.)

And they have very deep meanings
      – unless not.
(Maybe they're just random feelings?)

Some even have exclamation marks!
      And some are "Dedicated To . . ."
(but no Odes to Sharks!)

Some may explain things while some are confusing,
      as are those about politics – sorry –
(though some are amusing!)

Some may recount memories, others maybe dreams,
      some, mere bits of whimsy,
(one might be about flying machines!)

There are those for adults, and those for kids
      but definitely not all –
(for adults that is.)

Some may make you painfully aware,
      others will make you want to *$#%!
(fume and swear.)

Some may lift you up, others let you down
      some will make you smile –
(but not one has a clown.)

And you may feel your heart melt,
      if I tell you,
(shh: they're all heartfelt.)

So you know the drill: some are glad,
        some are sad,
(no need to ponder and mope.)

Overall, good poems are just . . . good poems.
        I could say "or whatever",
but there's more meaning to them
        than that – (I hope.)

How It Goes

Ignorance is Ignorance.
> *Sometimes unavoidable, and then forgivable too;*
> *Often frustrating, but what else can you do?*

Willful Ignorance is Arrogance.
> *Enshrining Myth at the expense of what's True,*
> *Then demanding conformity and following suit.*

Willful Arrogance sublimates into Fascism.
> *Welcome to the world of obsequious Democracy,*
> *And leading the way, Congressional complacency.*

Willful Fascism embraces a Tyrant.
> *Wave goodbye to domestic tranquility,*
> *Say hello to political obscenity.*

Loyalty becomes the Tyrants obsession.
> *There's power in spewing conspiracy and division,*
> *And attacking opponents with lies and derision.*

Latent insecurities demand a fisted iron hand,
> *Making oneself seem, as so very strong*
> *Never caring about what's right or wrong*

until there is no longer any law of the land.
> *All, all attained through the morbid propensity*
> *Of an abject lack of respect for fact –*
> *And invariably for a Nation, a fatal prophecy.*

Ode to Daily Routine

I get up in the morning while still dark,
so I can tend to the plants in the park –
and stop the meowing of the cat who is prowling
wanting to know when his breakfast will start.

Next I get the paper from off the front lawn,
charge up the phone and check that the coffee is on.
I'll listen to the news while tying my shoes,
grab a cuppa joe, out the door, and I'm gone.

Now there's a reason for this middling routine:
it's the time honored sequence that cranks-up the machine;
which starts the motor that turns the rotor
that spins the planet, thus getting the day to begin.

It may seem such little things to turn the Earth on its axis,
but it's a hefty responsibility – that's why they call me Atlas.

Jigsaws

We set the table up and pull the old box down
open it up, turn it over and splay the parts around,
with lots of anticipation – and a little trepidation –
we marvel at the colors and the funny shapes we've found.

Some begin by sorting pieces, piling them up as if on mission
searching for meaningful words or faces in facets weirdly misshapen.
Others seek out special shapes, as those that have their edges straight
hoping a border will bring at least a beginning of comprehension.

The puzzles can bring out a fond reminiscence,
reminding us of particular places and previous events
such as rainy day cabins and old family gatherings:
then into the task we dive, trying to make it make sense.

Holding that this piece here, should fill that empty space,
yet we find its perfect partner with another, in another place.
So many parts that just won't fit, but doggedly we ply away at it,
past matches, mismatches and gaps until finally it takes its shape.

As the frame is complete and the jaggedy picture appears
an anxiousness pervades the air, now we see the end is near.
Some contentedly stand aside – while others of us desperately try –
to connect together the jigsaw puzzle pieces of our lives.

Ode to Cernan

(And The Others)

He was the twelfth and last man to walk off the moon,
and in one giant step for a man, too soon
he sighed as his left foot lifted from its dusty perch,
swung in an arc, and landed back on Earth.
Mission Apollo was over far and away before its time,
one fleeting step back, for all mankind.

The Man in the Moon watched warily, and unseen by them
duffled his dreams, slid up the steps and slipped inside the LEM.
He left behind the Rabbit because he wanted to find out,
how real gravity felt, and what that blue was all about.
He wanted to breathe air under skies he'd barely seen,
and understand the intricacies of the color green.

But now at night, deep in slumber, do each their spirits hover over,
searching for the moon in the man on the face of the other?

Black Holes I Have Known

My bank account.

A pair of Danish blue eyes.

The business end of a 38.

That particular song.

Rejected submissions.

A second Tarot reading – worse that the first (and both came true).

Disappointing someone who had faith in you.

Grief.

Depression.

Staring into one long cold cup of coffee.

An end.

Of Mystery and Substance

I.
Martiene the Magnificent

He dances around a ball of light
throwing shadows into the mist,
a bond of life being built
in exquisite evanescence.

His hands shake and rattle in the midnight air,
making maraca-cans clank in rustic ritual.
He raises and sprays here, then there,
adding yet more of the pungent chemical.

And all the time he's humming to himself
seemingly mumbling incantations.
Figures emerge from the vaporous shelf:
a crown, a miter, a crenelation.

As if from the mists of a glistening stream
his hand draws forth a horse.
He sets it on edge in harness to its team,
and there it's given a life-long purpose!

Now on that board of burl and mesquite,
apple-wood kings and queens seemingly slumber,
while in their dreams do they ready to compete
with the opposites of their number?

Thinking they'll cross that field with sword and shield
striding forth as sovereign conquerors;
yet they will awake on that checkered slate
merely pawns in the hands of unseen conjurers.

II.
Steve's Garage

Come with me now to Steve's garage
and see his handiwork in the backyard,
where the building leans on doors open wide,
with a cavernous dark nestled inside.

Now that the overhead work light is off
step round where spray-paint cans were tossed
– watch out for a vise or a rusty wrench –
come right on up to the carpenter's bench.

Here in the dawn light the figures seem to glow
with the patina of care that the craftsman bestowed.
Each one unique and now neatly arrayed,
see how they shine, their parts ready to play!

Ah, that our place in the Universe be so understood
as these little chessmen carved out of wood.

Some Mornings!

And God got up in a bit of a grump, on the Second Day.
He'd tossed and turned while His mind had churned
worrying about the job that still ahead of Him lay.
He rubbed a rib that still was sore from all the work the day before,
musing, *"I've got to get rid of this pain some way."*

But His cat gave a wail when He stepped on its tail –
startled! – He leapt back; then heard *that* rib crack,
as He lost His balance and onto a table He fell.
He grumbled and mumbled, as into the kitchen He stumbled
and into a puddle of – what? – even He couldn't tell.

He then stubbed His toe while looking high and low,
and began muttering things, not quite so lofty;
slamming cabinets and drawers and pantry doors
He finally shouted out: *"Where in Hell is the damn coffee?!"*

The Church of the Flying Tube

      We sit in shortened pews,
and wait as the Stewards go through
      the motions of blessing,
a sort of two arm general
      genuflection –
side to side, up and down, to the back
      and then the front;
should we feel the pressure of need
      they point up,
to wherein sustenance will fall like manna
      and relief bestow.
Or find under your seat salvation
      from what lies
in the unknown down below.
      Be assured
that extra prayers may into a tube
      be blown.

      Once the liturgy takes flight,
the taking of wafers and of placating sips
      offer surety and respite.
Later will be the passing of donation bags
      for all you've been given,
asking for you to offer in return that,
      of which you have riven.

During the course there are those who read,
      and those who play,
some who sing silently and some
      who pray –
especially when the winds of our fate
      storm and howl
shaking the falseness out of serenity and
      urning stomachs foul.

All are waiting for the culmination. All are ready
      to stand by
to receive redemption of their faith, in the unseen
      pilot of the sky,
whose reassuring voice told us of the wheres
      and whys
of how far we'll go and how high
      we'll fly
before the time that will inevitably
      come 'round
to what we can expect when we
      go to ground.

Once heaven and earth are no longer
      in contention
relieved we receive the final
      benediction
and as we file out showing grimace
      or grin,
some mutter fond salutations
    and others a well meant
        "Amen".

The Blackened Heart of Hypocrisy
I.
Sixteenth St.

Four middle aged men, furtive and grinning
    each with sticks of doom.
Four little girls in a House of the Lord
    Blown to smithereens.

Take a quick look at each group of four,
    so interestingly similar:
they attended churches, prided themselves
    on their Charity,
on their Patriotism, and no doubt
    their Heritage too.
Yet so despairingly different it makes
    you wonder about a God.

Four men to set 'em in – but there were more:
    the ones who sold it,
the ones who bought it, the ones
    who drove it, who
slapped them on the back on their way
    to the little girl's sanctuary,
and again after they'd laid in the sticks
    and again after they'd
lit 'em off, and blew four little girls
    to Kingdom Come.

II.

Forging Chains

And their raised glasses went "clink"
    but it was really a "clank"
as another link was forged in the chain of evil
    that wrapped around their necks.

And the preacher said, "God is Love"
    but made a wink,
only it made the sound of "chunk",
    as another link was forged
in the chain that would drag him to Hell
    and bind him there.

And the wife says to the children
    "Your father murdered
some girls today!" And they might ask,
    "Mama, was that brave?"
And when she replies, "Oh yes I think" ... "Chank,"
    another link
in the chain of hate is wrapped
    around their souls.

III.

Blackened Hearts

There are the little hypocrisies which we allow –
say, when we accuse others of things we have done.
But if left unchecked the little white lies grow
and zealots and politicians begin a free run.
When they see they can bend the moral fiber once,
then they'll try it again with a little tweak next,
and yet again if we still give them a pass;
then even more until it becomes a continual test.
Hypocrisy then comes into a Being of its own,
that controls everything it can touch.
From the national, to the state, to the pulpit
and home, and into the hearts of the ones it will crush.
And little men plant their blackened thoughts
to reap a crop of bitterness and sorrow.
Seeking the death of a Child or a House of God,
seeking to tear this country apart,
seeking a society corrupt and immoral.

How a Ghost Sees Things

I blend in and then out among the fog and mists
everything, it seems is so damned vaporous,
which makes my existence a constant horror
when I can't even see myself in a mirror.

It's awfully hard to grasp things, not just objects
but even the most simplest of ideas and concepts
such as, *Where am I?*, or, *What is that?*, yet nothing is clear.
The questions drift off unanswered, and I'm still here.

As for sustenance I'm actually OK, you see
the vapors from empty bottles belong to me.
The same is true of the sizzles from a grill
or the aromas wafting from a baker's window sill.

The Hell of it is I still reach out to grab and snatch
only to hit a mental wall with a soul shaking smack!
And I have to face up, over and over, yet again
I'm not here at all, and fade back, away, just a whim.

I can't stand the sun, though I don't know why.
Can't stand any water, makes me want to cry.
Can't stand the night, though I can finally be seen
sometimes, in the misty vapors of your dreams.

Don't know why I'm putting this into those wisps,
I can't write anything down in them, and you can't read it.

Parisian Orpheunium

Way down under in the catacombs
the wind courses coldly whispering over bones,
and the skeletal skulls that stare without sight
are damp and chill in the flickering light.

A little bit above rumble the *Metro's* subway trains,
whooshing musty air down their tunneled lanes.
Strap hanging passengers dressed in long winter blacks
sway silently to a rickety-rack of staccato tracks.

Then they bustle up the stairs or take an escalator,
past Ukrainian buskers and a Gypsy beggar.
The crowd surges out to an unaccustomed sight –
the clouds have finally parted and the sun is shining bright!

Flower stalls are opening – Springtime has arrived:
People shed their dreary coats and Paris comes alive!

Poetry Webinair

I.
UT's HRC

They have Poetry on the Plaza
on the University's selected day,
during the semesters' seasons
from September until May.

The readers' words float upwards
soaring off into the sky,
trying to catch an intense thought
or a curious slice of life.

For poetry is the distillation
of the moment when everything turns,
spiraling out to latch onto,
and then encase, an idea's germ.

But my own little dawn of realization
on this day when the breeze is fair,
is the Black Widows' yearly migration,
      has taken to the air.

II.
You See:

When some mysterious signal is given
they cast their strands up and away,
then ride their webs on the gusting wind –
and they're sailing over the Plaza on this
      warm and blustery day.

III.
You'll See:

Their silvr'y strands glinting in the sun
as they float by overhead,
ensnaring the words, thoughts and deeds
of poets long thought dead.

When the Widow feels some soft vibration
will she stealthily move in for the kill,
only to find her incisive venom
no match for the writer's quill?

Yet still flying away with those purloined phrases
which in this rising gale is hard to hear,
and since I barely catch snatches of faraway places,
I too am off, to find a niche and wrap my hands
        around an ice-cold beer.

When It's Gettin' Hot in Texas

Well, when it's getting' hot in Texas
and climbs past 90 degrees
you can bet your boots spring has sprung
and there won't be another freeze.

Now your own body's temperature
is around ninety-eight-point-six,
and as a thermometer rises up
your sweat begins to fizz.

And a funny thing happens when that heat
goes up and past your own –
your body well melt, your hands will float
and you'll think your mind has flown.

And as that outside temp keeps climbing
and goes past ahunert and eight,
a funny thing happens in that heat –
your soul can evaporate.

It's a phenomenon not unknown to man
so be careful of triple digits,
if you don't hang on to your shadow's grip
you're in danger of losing it.

Now some say the same thing happens
when you're hiking out on treks,
or if you've been running a marathon mile
and you're deep into your klicks.

The difference with the heat is,
sometimes you don't even know
until the chills come over you –
that's when Death will swoop in low

You desperately need to find a way
to cool your body down,
for if there is no water or shade
you might end up underground.

And sometimes there's just nothing,
no, nothing close at hand.
You can fall on your knees, beg the Lord please
but you're headed for the promised land.

Yet there's a way to keep your soul intact –
just stop your forlorn quest,
and laugh at this cosmic joke called life
'cause laughter, my friend, is the cooling-est.

With a Wink

To the British a nod is as good as a wink;
      but there's much more to it
than that – I think.

A nod may be, in its primal essence,
      simple acknowledgment
of another's presence.

But it's also a kind of binding sentience,
      that lets others know
when all are in agreement:

a nod among those who's hands have a hold,
      gives the signal for
the old 'heave-ho!';

it grants recognition to right of position
      and gives the go at a crossing,
or makes a bid at an auction.

To working strangers whose backs are bent
      it gauges their labor
with a compliment.

To others on society's outskirts
      it communes with their frustration
underlined with a smirk.

A nod to a lady may grant a bit of grace
      in a reciprocal smile
that lights up her face.

Nods to acquaintances you pass in the street;
      to drivers and bikers and cops on the beat;
and to those you see but with which don't wish to speak.

Or it's signals between siblings across a room
        as elders pontificate
on today's proliferate, gloom and doom.

It's a way to loved ones permission is given
        with a sigh,
as the Old Folks just . . . give in.

It brings arguments to conclusion,
        puts plotters in collusion,
with the skullduggery they're plotting up next.

With a twinkle, it smooths a wrinkle
        to things, not quite so simple,
in matters pertaining with the opposite sex.

A nod is the sign to let the music begin,
        all this and more
          – amen!

In all these things it grants an acceptance
        in a motion
of mutual acquiescence.

Compare that quick down and up motion
to a sewing machine and its "bob" –
maybe our society is knit together
        with little more than
the underappreciated, almost reflexive,
        seemingly inconsequential,
                nod.

Cornucopias I Have Known

Laundry baskets.

                    Mail boxes.

An infant's mother's purse.

Spring.

The road.

My wife's heart.

Things Return to Place

It can start at the end of a party,
a birthday, a broadcast, a *"bon voyage"*.
Too late, too tired to clean – to bed! "Leave it",
laughingly, "for tomorrow's *'le garbagge'*".
Next day pick up, sweep up, dishes washed,
leftovers wrapped up, frozen or tossed.
Dumping the cups and urns filled with ash,
then sorting the glasses and cans from the back.
And when the tableware is back in its case,
finally a restful minute, a bit of contentment,
      that things have returned to place.

Or it can happen in the middle of a day,
when some time alone with others away.
On the radio you'll hear a familiar tune
that takes you back, to a roll in the sack
with a lover you'd long forgot.
What if, you begin to wonder and presume;
then the music stops – whether wanted or not –
and you're staring a mirror hard in the face.
You've come back from the moon, all too soon
      and sigh, as you return to place.

And it can end at the start of a sunset sky,
out on the porch rocking side by side.
In the starry vastness soaring birds cry;
we take each other's hand, I understand,
      there's no reason to ask why:
Did we do as we should?
Did we raise the kids good?
No, not always but we tried
as memories well up in our eyes.
By luck or by fate, we found God's grace,
from the witnessing of birth, to this calling Earth,
serene now in the knowledge that things,
      return to place.

The End

Eugene writes this to you from Austin Texas and hopes that in these poems you may have found something to think about, or that you can empathize with, or that has given you a smile, or even just a bit of peace.
Thanks – E.C.

www.ingramcontent.com/pod-product-compliance
Lightning Source LLC
Chambersburg PA
CBHW030203100526
44592CB00009B/418